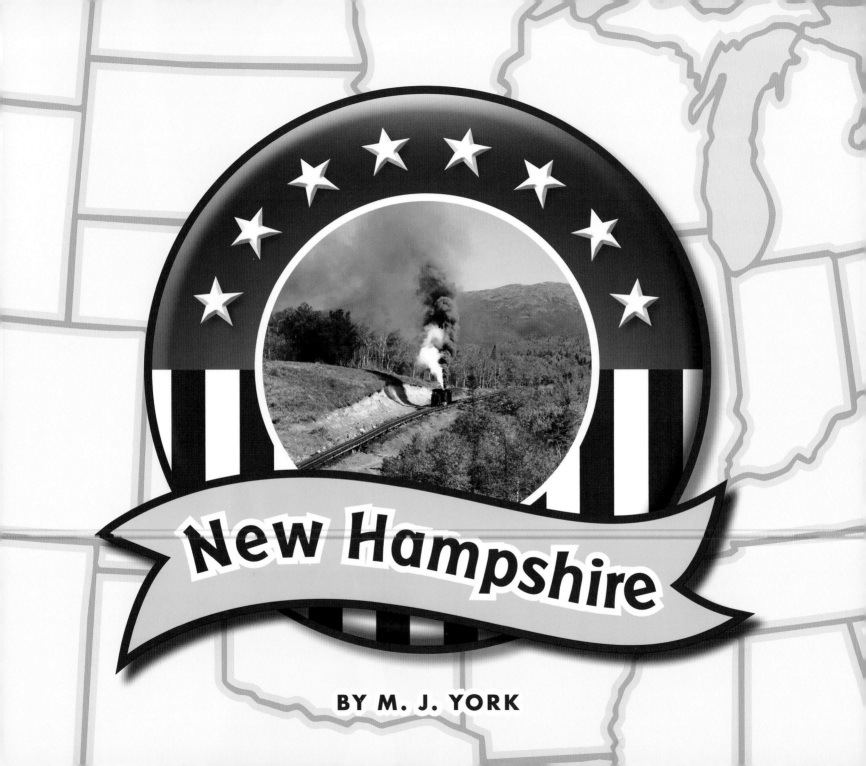

New Hampshire

BY M. J. YORK

The Child's World

Published by The Child's World®
1980 Lookout Drive • Mankato, MN 56003-1705
800-599-READ • www.childsworld.com

ACKNOWLEDGMENTS
The Child's World®: Mary Berendes, Publishing Director
The Design Lab: Design and production
Red Line Editorial: Editorial direction

PHOTO CREDITS: Big Stock Photo, cover, 1, 3; Matt Kania/Map Hero, Inc.,
4, 5; Denis Jr. Tangney/iStockphoto, 7, 13; Galina Mushinsky/Bigstock, 9;
iStockphoto, 10; Julia Freeman-Woolpert/Bigstock, 11; North Wind Picture
Archives, 15; Chee-On Leong/iStockphoto, 17; AP Images, 19; Michael
Shake/iStockphoto, 21; One Mile Up, 22; Quarter-dollar coin image from
the United States Mint, 22

LIBRARY OF CONGRESS CATALOGING-IN-PUBLICATION DATA
York, M. J., 1983–
  New Hampshire / by M.J. York.
      p. cm.
  Includes index.
  ISBN 978-1-60253-473-5 (library bound : alk. paper)
  1. New Hampshire—Juvenile literature. I. Title.

  F34.3.Y67 2010
  974.2—dc22

                                        2010019191

Printed in the United States of America in Mankato, Minnesota.
July 2010
F11538

On the cover: A train
makes its way up
New Hampshire's
Mount Washington.

CONTENTS

Geography

Let's explore New Hampshire! New Hampshire is in the northeastern United States. This area is called New England.

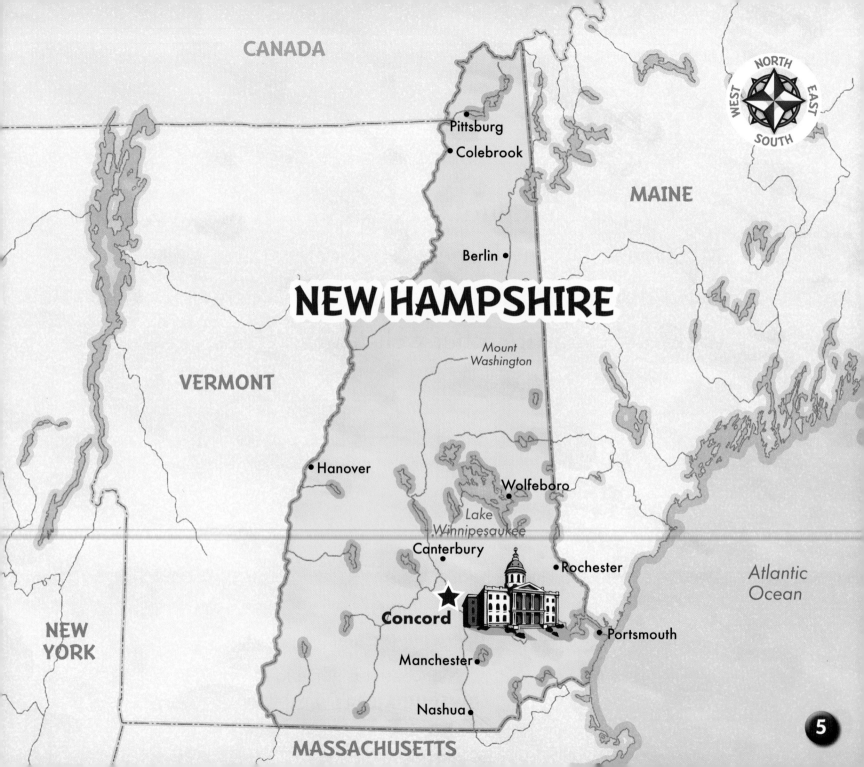

CANADA

NORTH
WEST   EAST
SOUTH

• Pittsburg

• Colebrook

MAINE

Berlin •

NEW HAMPSHIRE

Mount
Washington

VERMONT

• Hanover

• Wolfeboro

Lake
Winnipesaukee

Canterbury •

• Rochester

NEW
YORK

Concord

Atlantic
Ocean

• Portsmouth

Manchester •

Nashua •

MASSACHUSETTS

Cities

Concord is the capital of New Hampshire. Manchester is the largest city in the state. It is home to about 110,000 people. Nashua and Rochester are other well-known cities.

Manchester is home to libraries, **museums**, and many businesses. ▶

Land

New Hampshire has many hills and mountains. It is famous for its hills made of **granite**. New Hampshire has 18 miles (29 km) of coastline on the Atlantic Ocean. Lake Winnipesaukee is a large lake in the state.

New Hampshire is called "the Granite State."

New Hampshire has **lighthouses** along its rocky coast. ▶

Plants and Animals

Forests cover most of New Hampshire. These areas are known for beautiful fall colors. The state tree is the white birch. New Hampshire's state bird is the purple finch. Its state animal is the white-tailed deer. The state wildflower is the pink lady's slipper. It grows in forests.

The pink lady's slipper became New Hampshire's state wildflower in 1991. ▶

People and Work

More than 1.3 million people live in New Hampshire. Some people make machines and **technology** products. Many other people work in jobs that serve tourists. Some people farm. Apples, potatoes, eggs, and maple syrup are important New Hampshire products.

Portsmouth is home to a large shipyard where ships are repaired. ▶

History

People from England built a **colony** in the New Hampshire area in 1623. New Hampshire was one of the original 13 colonies that became the first 13 U.S. states. In 1776, New Hampshire became the first colony to adopt its own state **constitution**. In 1788, New Hampshire became the ninth state.

New England colonists walk along a town street. ▶
New Hampshire was named after Hampshire, England.

Ways of Life

People visit New Hampshire to see the leaves change color in the fall. They come to ski in the winter. The first ski club in the country was founded here in 1882.

Many people enjoy winter sports in New Hampshire. ▶

Famous People

Poet Robert Frost lived in New Hampshire and other New England states. Franklin Pierce was born in New Hampshire. He was the fourteenth U.S. president. Alan B. Shepard Jr. was the first American in outer space. He was also born in New Hampshire.

Robert Frost won many prizes for his poetry. ▶

Famous Places

Mount Washington is in New Hampshire. It is the highest mountain in New England. It reaches 6,288 feet (1,917 m). The state is famous for the Old Man of the Mountain. It was a **formation** in granite on a mountainside. It was shaped like an old man's face. The granite fell off the mountain in 2003.

New Hampshire is known for its natural beauty. ▶

The fastest wind ever recorded in the United States was at Mount Washington in 1934. The wind reached 231 miles per hour (372 km/h).

State Symbols

Seal

The state seal of New Hampshire shows a **frigate**. This ship is named *Raleigh*. It was built in New Hampshire. It was used during a battle of the **American Revolution**. Go to childsworld.com/links for a link to New Hampshire's state Web site, where you can get a firsthand look at the state seal.

Flag

New Hampshire's state flag shows the state seal. The state **motto** of New Hampshire is "Live free or die." A leader of the American Revolution first said it.

Quarter

New Hampshire's state quarter shows an image of the Old Man of the Mountain. The quarter came out in 2000.

Glossary

American Revolution (uh-MER-ih-kin rev-uh-LOO-shun): During the American Revolution, from 1775 to 1783, the 13 American colonies fought against Britain for their independence. A famous boat from New Hampshire was used during a battle of the American Revolution.

colony (KOL-uh-nee): A colony is an area of land that is newly settled and is controlled by a government of another land. The English built a colony in the New Hampshire area in 1623.

constitution (kon-stuh-TOO-shun): A constitution is a document that has laws about how a state or country is governed. New Hampshire was the first colony to adopt its own state constitution.

formation (for-MAY-shun): A formation is a shape that appears in something. There was a stone formation in New Hampshire that looked like an old man.

frigate (fri-GET): A frigate is a type of ship. A frigate appears on New Hampshire's state seal.

granite (GRAN-it): Granite is a type of hard rock. New Hampshire is known as "the Granite State."

lighthouses (LYT-howss-ez): Lighthouses are tall buildings near oceans or large lakes that use lights to warn ships of danger. New Hampshire has lighthouses along its coast.

motto (MOT-oh): A motto is a sentence that states what people stand for or believe. The state motto of New Hampshire is "Live free or die."

museums (myoo-ZEE-umz): Museums are places where people go to see art, history, or science displays. Visitors can see museums in Manchester.

seal (SEEL): A seal is a symbol a state uses for government business. New Hampshire's seal has a famous ship on it.

symbols (SIM-bulz): Symbols are pictures or things that stand for something else. The seal and flag are symbols of New Hampshire.

technology (tek-NAWL-uh-jee): Technology is scientific knowledge applied to practical things. Some people in New Hampshire work to make technology products.

Further Information

Books

Harris, Marie. *G is for Granite: A New Hampshire Alphabet*. Chelsea, MI: Sleeping Bear Press, 2002.

Keller, Laurie. *The Scrambled States of America*. New York: Henry Holt, 2002.

Ribke, Simone T. *New Hampshire*. New York: Children's Press, 2003.

Web Sites

Visit our Web site for links about New Hampshire: *childsworld.com/links*

Note to Parents, Teachers, and Librarians: We routinely verify our Web links to make sure they are safe and active sites. So encourage your readers to check them out!

Index